performed by **Neil Sedaka**   illustrated by **Tim Bowers**

DINOSAUR PET

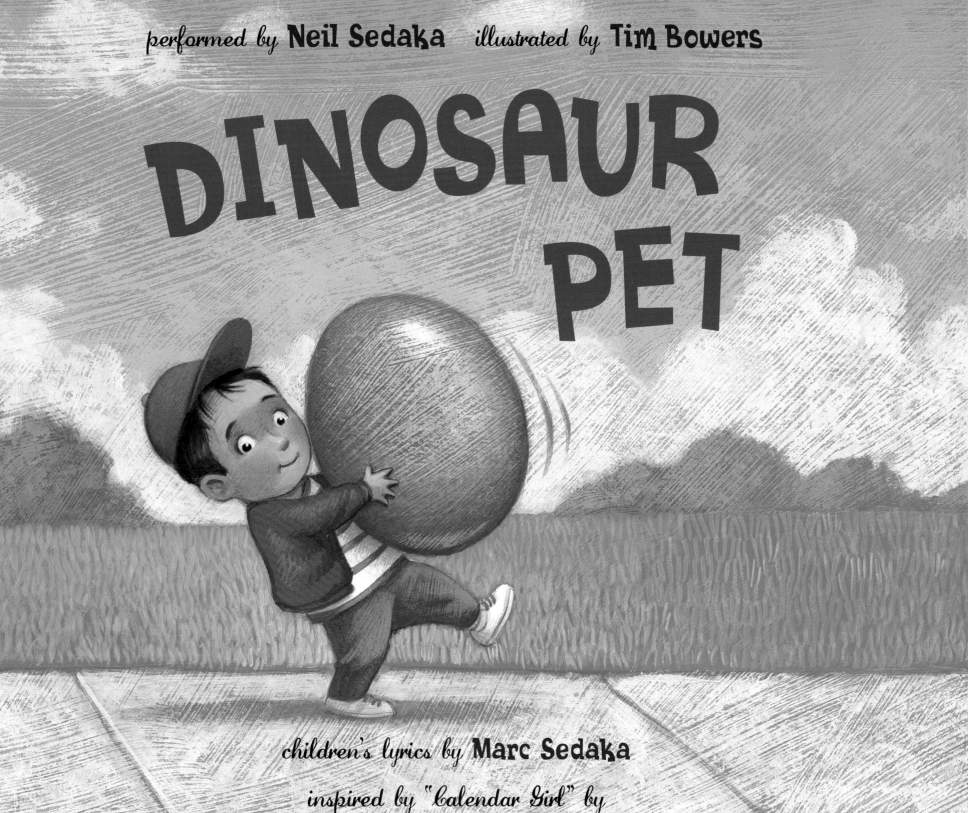

children's lyrics by **Marc Sedaka**

inspired by "Calendar Girl" by
Neil Sedaka & Howard Greenfield

imagine!
Publishing

I love, I love, I love
my dinosaur pet.
Yeah, sweet dinosaur pet.

I love, I love, I love
my dinosaur pet.
Each and every day of the year.

January,
he's **breaking out**
of his shell.

February,

his body's starting to swell.

March,

at least **eight times a day**
he's got to be fed.

April,

when he sleeps with me he **crushes the bed.**

Yeah, yeah, how big
can he get?

I **love**, I **love**, I **love**
my little dinosaur pet.

Every day, **every day**, every day,
every day of the year,
Every day of the year.

May,

maybe if the roof was
twice as tall.

June,

he wouldn't bump it when
he's **roaming the hall.**

July,
like the fireworks,
he touches the sky.

August,

the cost of groceries is **bleeding us dry.**

Yeah, yeah, how big
can he get?

I love, I love, I love
my little dinosaur pet.

Every day, every day, every day,
every day of the year,
Every day of the year.

Yeah, yeah, how big
can he get?

I love, I love, I love
my little dinosaur pet.

Every day, every day, every day,
every day of the year,
Every day of the year.

September,
just the tail alone is
thirty feet long.

October,

when we trick or treat
he goes as King Kong.

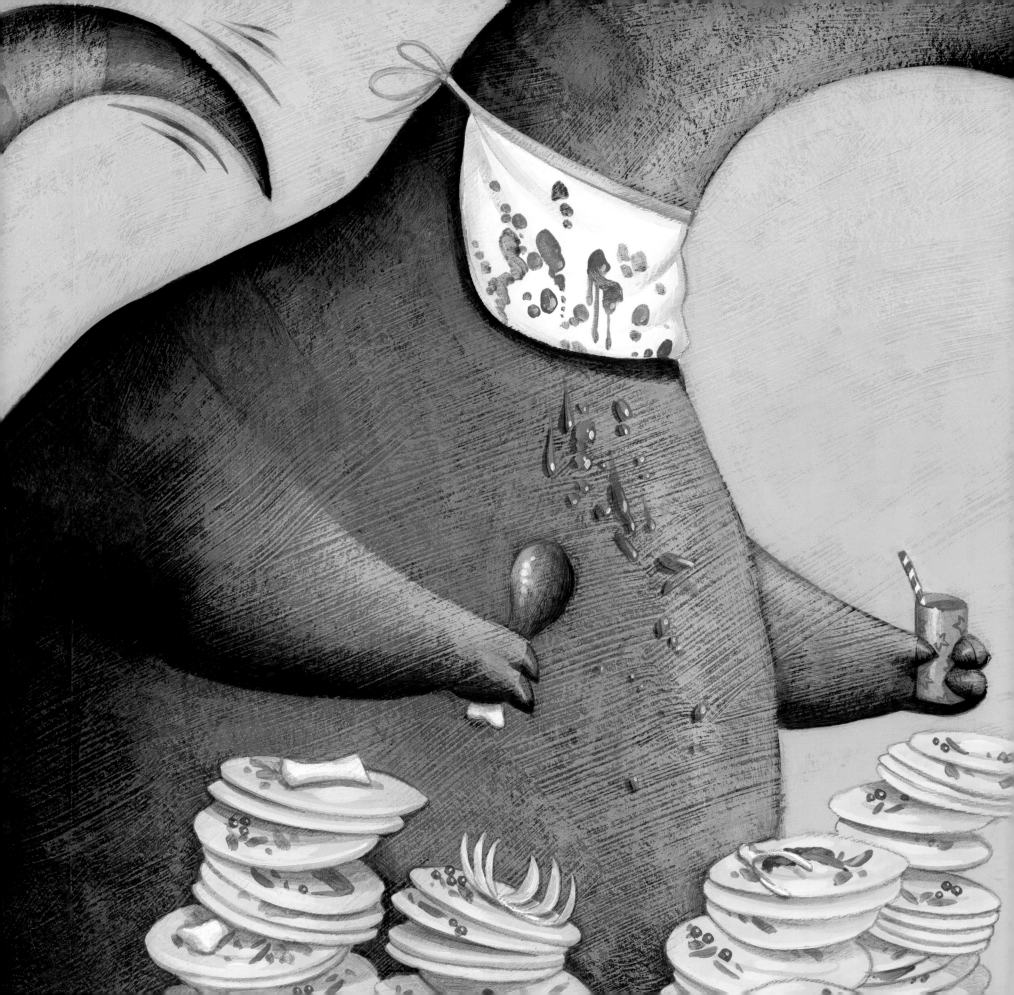

November,
fifty turkeys
weren't nearly enough.

Yeah, yeah, how big
can he get?

I love, I love, I love
my little dinosaur pet.

December,

come the new year things are **gonna get rough.**

Every day, **every day**, every day,
every day of the year,
Every day of the year.

I love, I love, I love
my dinosaur pet.
Yeah, sweet dinosaur pet.

I love, I love, I love
my dinosaur pet.
Yeah, sweet dinosaur pet.

I love, I love, I love
my dinosaur pet.
Yeah, sweet dinosaur pet.

I love, I love, I love
my dinosaur pet.

Performer's Note

This is our second children's book in hopefully a series of many. On this book, I collaborated with my son Marc Sedaka, who wrote the new lyric to the original tune of "Calendar Girl," my hit record from 1961. My five-year-old grandson Michael is a dinosaur fanatic, and it was he who inspired the book. I hope you also enjoy the three-song CD, which includes "Dinosaur Pet" and two brand-new Neil Sedaka songs: "She Moved Away" and "The Tooth Fairy." I am delighted that I am now reaching the young generation of book readers, after the success of *Waking Up Is Hard to Do*. Please enjoy the story and the songs.

Illustrator's Note

Songs can remind us of people and places throughout our lives. Neil Sedaka's songs are attached to many fond memories from my earlier years, growing up in Ohio. Now, a new generation will build memories together with familiar songs to mark those special times, and once again, Neil Sedaka's songs will help mark memories. I'm so glad to be able to contribute the artwork that will accompany his wonderful music. With the recent arrival of our first grandchild, my wife and I look forward to sharing a chorus of "I love, I love, I love my dinosaur pet" and the great memories it will create for years to come.

Library of Congress Cataloging-in-Publication Data is Available

An Imagine Book
Published by Charlesbridge
85 Main Street
Watertown, MA 02472
617-926-0329
www.charlesbridge.com

Children's Lyrics by Marc Sedaka
Illustrated by Tim Bowers
Inspired by "Calendar Girl" by Howard Greenfield
and Neil Sedaka
Performed by Neil Sedaka

For my grandchildren Charlotte,
Amanda, and Michael. —NS

To my grandson, Caleb. —TB